AF485152

All About the 15 Famous Greek Philosophers

Biography History Books Children's Historical Biographies

BABY PROFESSOR

EDUCATION KIDS

Speedy Publishing LLC
40 E. Main St. #1156
Newark, DE 19711
www.speedypublishing.com

Copyright 2017

All Rights reserved. No part of this book may be reproduced or used in any way or form or by any means whether electronic or mechanical, this means that you cannot record or photocopy any material ideas or tips that are provided in this book

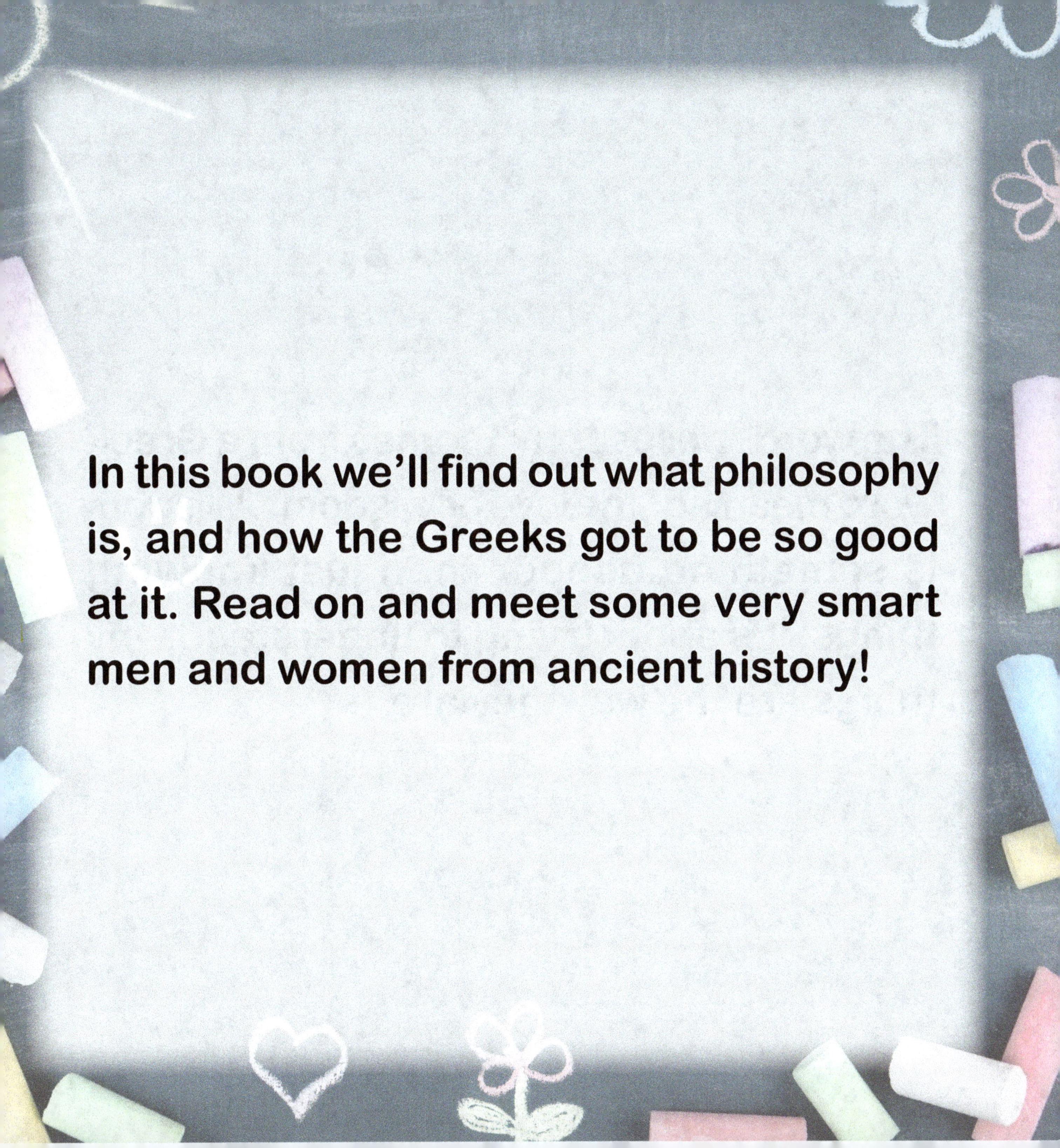

In this book we'll find out what philosophy is, and how the Greeks got to be so good at it. Read on and meet some very smart men and women from ancient history!

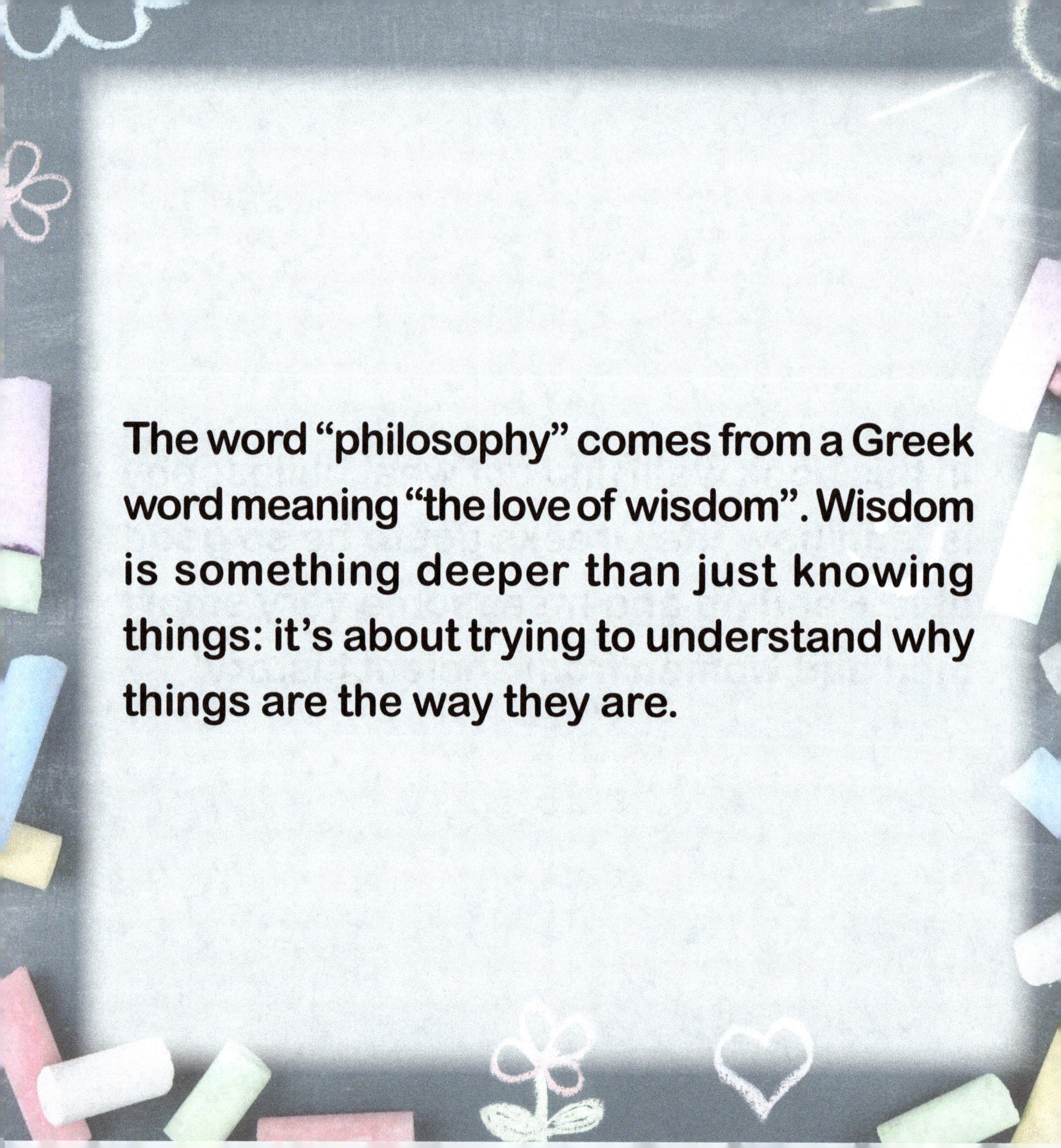

The word "philosophy" comes from a Greek word meaning "the love of wisdom". Wisdom is something deeper than just knowing things: it's about trying to understand why things are the way they are.

If you look at the world around you, you can learn many things. You can see that mothers and fathers love their babies, even though the babies take a lot of work and effort and don't seem to be any use to anybody. But if you start to ask, "Why do parents love their babies?", you are moving beyond collecting information to a philosophical question: why?

Philosophy might seem like some kind of exercise professors work at, but we all face philosophical questions. Here are three you face every day of your life: What makes me, me? Why am I here? How should I shape my life?

People have been asking questions like this since we started using words, but it was only with the rise of the Greek philosophical tradition that the asking of questions started to produce useful answers.

The Story of Greek Philosophy

Greek philosophy developed during the sixth century BCE and continued for about eight hundred years. It influenced philosophical and practical thought in Europe and the Middle East, and in both Christian and Islamic culture. Some of what the Greeks called "philosophy" we would now call scientific study, especially the study of plants, animals, weather, and the sky at night.

Many philosophers founded or taught in schools or "academies", which were an important part of Greek cultural life. If you can imagine it, people would go to the academy to watch and hear people debate philosophy, with the same interest and excitement that we might have today when going to a rock concert.

15 Great Greek Philosophers

Here are some of the greatest Greek philosophers, from the oldest to the most recent. Most of them are men. That's not because women can't think about the big questions, but because in Classical times women got little respect as thinkers.

Thales (620 – 546 BCE)

People call Thales of Miletus the father of Ancient Greek philosophy. He looked into questions about the origin of matter, geography, mathematical equations, and the beginnings of the scientific method. He tried to develop a theory about why things grow and change, and he thought the basic element in the world was water.

THALES

Anaximander

Anaximander
(610 – 546 BCE)

Anaximander of Miletus was a student of Thales. He wrote about philosophical questions that included questions of geography and biology. He is the one of the first great astronomers, and tried to create a theory to explain how and why the whole universe exists.

Pythagoras (570 – 495 BCE)

We mainly think of Pythagoras as a mathematician, and we still use one of his theories to figure out the length of the long side of a right-angle triangle. He founded a famous school where he taught his approach to trying to understand the world, and offered rules of living to achieve a balanced life.

PYTHAGORAS.

Parmenides

Parmenides (510 – 560 BCE)

Parmenides was a student of Pythagoras, and was a poet as well as a philosopher. He wrestled with a basic question that he phrased "is it, or is it not?" He concluded that anything that "is" must always have been, and taught that nothing can come from nothing.

Anaxagoras (500 – 428 BCE)

Anaxagoras of Clazomenae worked as a teacher, scientist, and philosopher in Athens. He opposed traditional thinking that the actions of the Greek gods explained storms and earthquakes. He tried to understand, and explain, how everything in our world affects, and is affected by, other things. Anaxagoras taught that the universe was a single element, and that everything in the physical world included elements of every other thing.

Anaxagoras

Empedocles

Empedocles
(490 – 430 BCE)

Empedocles developed and taught the theory that every physical thing is made up of different proportions of the same four elements: earth, air, fire, and water. This was the standard assumption of all scientists in the western world for about two thousand years.

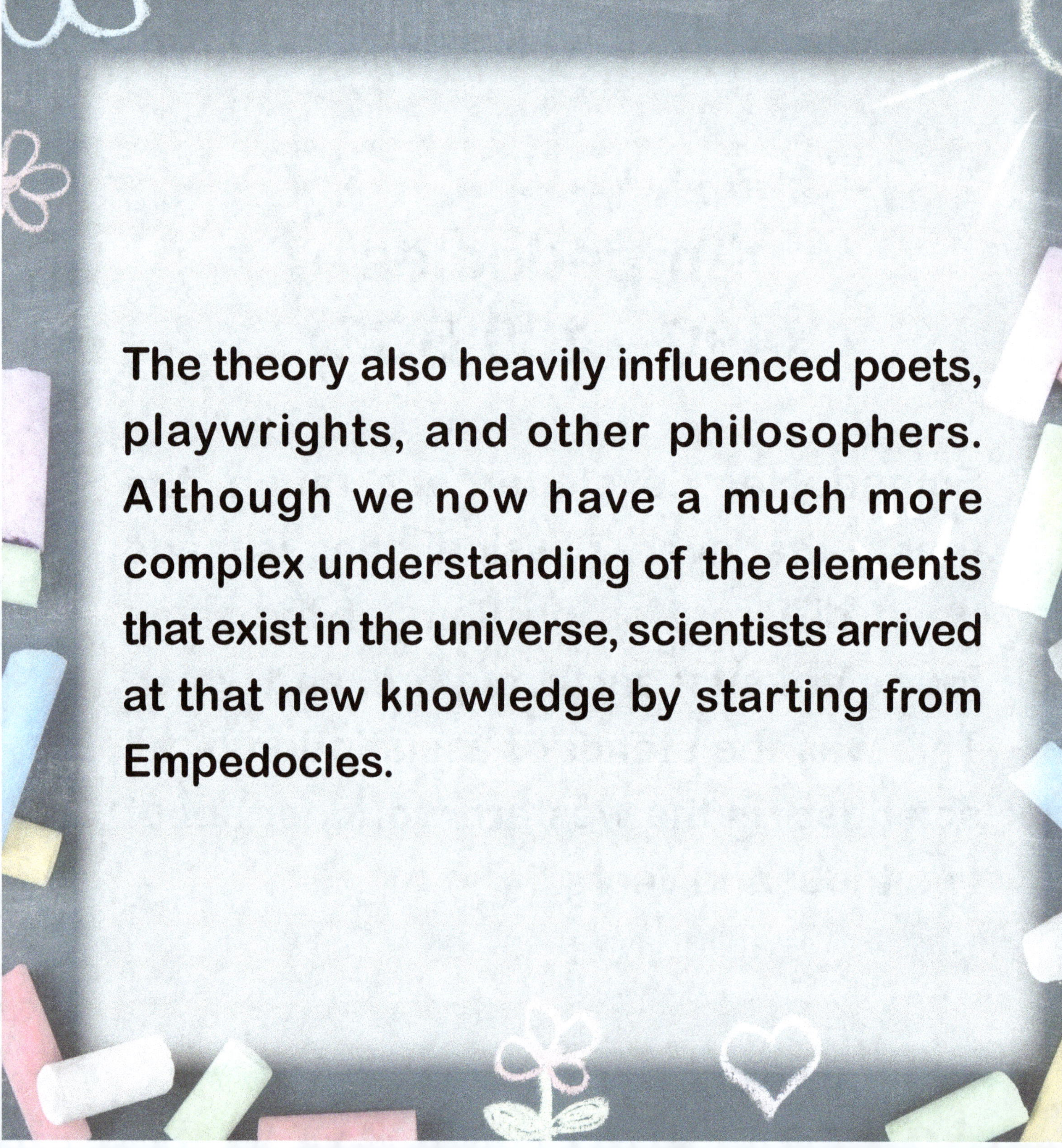

The theory also heavily influenced poets, playwrights, and other philosophers. Although we now have a much more complex understanding of the elements that exist in the universe, scientists arrived at that new knowledge by starting from Empedocles.

EMPIDOCLES
Raphael Sanctius Vrb. pinx. in aed. Vaticanis

Zeno

Zeno (490 – 430 BCE)

Zeno of Elea thought about what is bigger than the biggest number you can think of? What is one more than the most there is? He came up with the theory of infinity. Zeno tried to solve logical puzzles about the natural world, and to resolve ideas that contradicted each other.

As well as solving puzzles, Zeno proposed many himself that other philosophers wrestled with, such as "if everything that exists has a place, place too will have a place. Where is that place?" Another paradox was "a single grain of wheat doesn't make a sound when it falls, but a thousand grains falling together make a sound. How do a thousand nothings create a something?"

Aspasia

Aspasia (470 - 400 BCE)

Aspasia came to Athens from what is now Turkey. Her status as a foreigner meant she could be active in public life as Athenian women could not. Plato mentions her in his writings, and her teachings influenced Socrates.

Socrates (469 – 399 BCE)

Socrates offered a new method of approaching puzzling questions. He is famous for questioning everything, and then questioning the answer to the first question, and then questioning the answer to that. Often this process, the "Socratic Method", would lead to new insights or reveal that something that was thought to be "common knowledge" was based on an error or a prejudice.

Socrates

Socrates did not restrict himself to "safe" questions like where the sun goes when it is night. He questioned attitudes in society, why there should be soldiers, and why we should follow leaders. Powerful leaders in Athens felt threatened by Socrates' questions, and did not like him teaching his method to others. Finally he was put on trial for corrupting society, and was sentenced to death.

Democritus (460 –370 BC)

Some call Democritus the father of the modern scientific method. He pondered the nature of material things, and worked on developing the theory of atoms as the smallest building blocks of the physical world.

Democritus

Plato

Plato (427 – 347 BCE)

Plato was a student of Socrates who moved past his master in many ways while still honoring the work of his teacher and the Socratic Method. Plato considered questions of ethics, physics, and differences in language and accent between people.

He developed a theory we now describe as "Platonic absolutes": for instance, the courage a person has is a reflection and fragment of the absolute concept of courage. For Plato, the greatest absolute was "the good", and the greatest gain involves getting as close as possible to "the good" in morals, politics, and scientific study.

PLATO.

DIOGENES.

Diogenes (412 -323 BCE)

Diogenes of Sinope was a famous Cynic philosopher. Cynics held that the purpose of life is to live in virtue, in agreement with nature. They rejected trying to become wealthy or powerful, and taught instead that people should try to lead a simple life with as few possessions as possible.

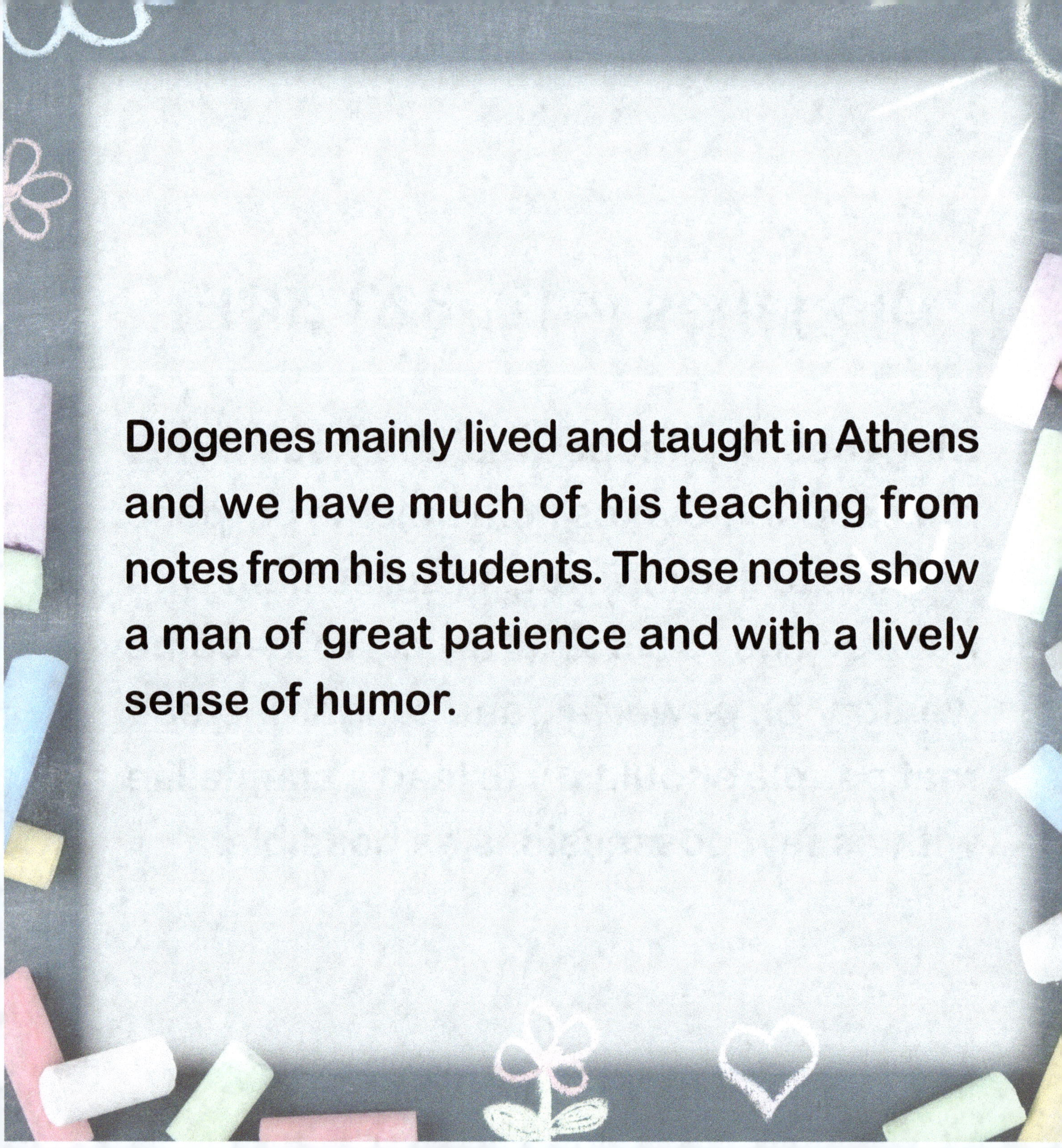

Diogenes mainly lived and taught in Athens and we have much of his teaching from notes from his students. Those notes show a man of great patience and with a lively sense of humor.

Sosipatra

Sosipatra (400-350 BCE)

Sosipatra was a philosopher and mystic who lived in Ephesus, in what is now Turkey. As a child, she learned Chaldean mystic teachings from two wise men. Remembering that women in that time and part of the world were not expected to take part in public life, it is interesting people said that her great wisdom made her husband seem small and inferior. As a widow, she moved to Pergamon and she taught many students who came to her academy.

Aristotle (384 – 322 BCE)

Aristotle is the best-known of Plato's students. He concentrated on discovery from personal experience, rather than learning from the writings of past masters. He was an inventive writer and investigator, and returned many times to subjects he had covered earlier, making new discoveries. He even laid down rules for what makes a good poem, or a good play, that structured writing and theater in Europe for two thousand years.

Aristotle

Aristotle served as tutor to a prince of Macedon who became Alexander the Great, conqueror of much of the known world. Their relationship was important for Alexander's development as a thoughtful ruler and not just a warrior king. It is also why we know much of what Aristotle taught, and how he spoke. His teachings spread through the whole of Alexander's empire, and then through all the Western and Middle-Eastern worlds.

Catherine of Alexandria (287 - 305 CE)

Catherine was a scholar who became a Christian at age 14 and helped bring many people to Christianity. She tried to show how Greek philosophy blended well with Christian teaching and life. She was executed by the emperor, who was not a Christian, for her efforts.

Catherine of Alexandria

Be a philosopher! The more you learn about the world and find out how and why things work, the more you are like one of the great Greek philosophers! Read on in other Baby Professor books and see what wonders you find!

Visit
BABY PROFESSOR
EDUCATION KIDS
www.BabyProfessorBooks.com
to download Free Baby Professor eBooks
and view our catalog of new and exciting
Children's Books

www.ingramcontent.com/pod-product-compliance
Lightning Source LLC
Chambersburg PA
CBHW060127120726
48003CB00009B/2800